ONCE UPON A WORLD is a new book presenting Bible stories for children in a unique, individual and highly-readable style. Stories selected from the old and new testaments are told in the modern idiom and illustrated with delightful cartoon sketches. An up-to-the-minute approach brings the stories vividly to life for the present generation, yet throughout Robert Duncan has retained a warmth and reverence for his subject. A happy combination of faith and humour has produced a book ideally suited to children of the nineteen-seventies.

ONCE UPON A WORLD is for families both remote from and close to the Christian faith, and will appeal equally to four and fourteen year olds, as well as to many perceptive adults.

Once Upon A World

A bedtime book of Bible stories
written and illustrated by
Robert Duncan

John Adams

Published by
JOHN ADAMS
Crazies Hill,
Wargrave, Berkshire, England.

First published in 1976

Made and printed in Great Britain
by Hunt Barnard Printing Ltd, Aylesbury.
Cover printed by Ferring Printing Company, Uxbridge.

To Charlotte

The publisher wishes to thank
Margaret Thomas, The Revd. D. G. A. Connor
and the Revd. J. W. Ratings, M.A., for their
contributions to the accuracy of this book.

Contents

THE NEW TESTAMENT

THE OLD TESTAMENT

THE CREATION

On the first day the world had ever known, God had a busy week in front of him. He said, 'We will have light and darkness, and I will call the light day, and the dark part night.' It all happened just as he said.

On the second day God decided there should be lots of sky all round the world. He called the sky Heaven. The next day he made all the land, and all the seas. He said that grass and plants and fruit would grow on the land.

On Thursday God worked a bit more on the light and darkness. He put finishing touches to it and threw in lots of stars. He was very pleased with what he had done.

The fifth day was very important for God. He made all the birds, and all the fishes. 'Have lots of children,' he told them. That's why there are so many birds in the sky and fishes in the sea.

He had a sleep, and the next morning he said, 'Today I shall make all the animals for the land, and if I have time I shall make a man, and he can be just like me.' He thought that was a very good idea.

By this time it was the world's seventh day – Sunday. God was very tired, he had worked hard for six whole days.

'I shall make this my day of rest,' he said.

And that's why we're all a bit lazy on Sundays.

ADAM AND EVE

When God had rested for a while, he got down to making the most beautiful garden. He called it the garden of Eden. It had wonderful trees, and flowers. It even had lots of birds and animals in it. Whatever your favourite animal is, it was there.

God put the man he had made into the garden. The man rubbed his eyes and looked all round. God said to him, 'Now listen, Adam (that was the man's name) you can eat the fruit, climb the trees, paddle in the rivers and jump over the bushes, but there's one thing you must never do. You must never eat the apples from the big tree in the middle of the garden, because that tree tells you what is good and what is bad.'

Adam said, 'What's bad?'

'Never mind,' said God, 'you go and have a nice time, and forget about that tree.'

God peeped out of the sky quite often to see how Adam was getting on, and soon he realised – Adam was lonely. God thought, 'he hasn't got any friends, no one to talk to – he will become unhappy soon.'

So one night, when Adam was asleep, God made a woman to be a friend for him. He called her Eve.

Adam and Eve got on very well together. They used to play with the animals, and eat lots of fruit from all the trees. Except one – the forbidden tree.

One day they decided to walk to the middle of the garden, and there was the most beautiful apple hanging from this special tree.

There was also a big nasty snake in the tree, who said, 'Hey, why don't you two eat that apple, it's the nicest, biggest, juiciest apple I ever saw.' Adam looked worried. 'We're not allowed to, God said so.'

'Oh, don't worry about that,' said the horrible snake. 'Have a bite, go on.'

Adam looked at Eve, and Eve looked at Adam, and the apple looked lovely. Eve tasted the apple.

'Go on, try it,' she said. Adam had a bite, and at once felt ashamed because he hadn't any clothes on.

It just happened that God was walking in the garden that day, and when Adam and Eve heard him coming up the path, they ran to hide.

God was very angry when he found them. 'You have eaten the fruit, haven't you?' he demanded. Adam said they had, but explained that the snake said it would be all right.

God told the snake that he was going to be the nastiest animal in the world, and he told Adam and Eve that now they would know everything about good and bad, for what good it would do them, and he turned them out of the garden of Eden and said they must look after themselves.

There was a great storm, and God went back to Heaven, leaving a flaming sword to make sure nobody touched the tree again.

NOAH'S ARK

Adam and Eve had sons, and their sons had sons, and the sons of the sons had sons. By that time there were lots of people on the world. God sat back and watched them. He saw them hurting each other, being selfish, and not thinking about him very much.

But God saw Noah, who was a very good man, and said, 'I like Noah, but I don't like the others much.'

The world had not turned out quite as well as he had hoped, so he decided to have a great storm, which would cause a flood, so he could start again. The flood would soon get rid of all the bad men, animals and everything that lived.

Before God started the storm he told Noah how to build a great boat – the ark. He told him how long it should be, how many rooms it should have, and how many windows and doors.

God said, 'Now listen, Noah, when your ark is finished, I want you to get two of every animal, two of every bird, and all the insects and bugs you can lay your hands on. Then get your wife, your sons, and their wives, and put the whole lot in the ark. Right?'

Noah said he would do it, and the ark was built. Just as the last nails were hammered in, the sky went black and the lightning started flashing. God had turned on the storm.

'Quick,' shouted Noah, 'everybody in. No pushing, you lions. Hurry up at the back, tortoises.'

Just in time, the door was shut and locked. For nearly six weeks it rained and rained and rained. All the ground was covered with water, and even the trees and mountains were covered.

But the ark sailed on. It bounced up and down a bit in the rough sea, but all the animals, all the birds, all the family, even old Noah, were safe and happy inside.

After a while the rain stopped banging on the roof, and sunlight started to shine through the cracks in the door and win-

dows. Noah knew it was time to find out if the water had gone down.

He thought, 'If I send out one of the doves it will soon tell me if there is any land showing yet.'

So that day, nearly a year after the ark had started its journey, Noah opened the window and the dove flew out into the clear blue sky. Noah looked round. He certainly couldn't see any land, just sea, sea, sea. (As far as he could see.) The dove came back looking a bit fed up. 'No good,' it said.

A week later, Noah sent out the dove again. This time it came flying back, proudly carrying an olive twig in its beak.

That told Noah the water had gone down enough for some land to appear, so he left it a few days and then opened the door of the ark. All the animals ran out on to the dry land; the horses prancing about, the kangaroos jumping up and down, and the lions growling happily.

They all thanked Noah for the lift, and went on their way.

God spoke to Noah. He said, 'I promise I won't flood the world again. Go now, and let all your children and grand-children make the world a really nice place to live in.'

God went away again, leaving a lovely rainbow to show that he was going to keep his promise.

ALL ABOUT JACOB

Hundreds of years later, after Noah's family had grown old, and all sorts of things had happened, Jacob and his brother Esau were born. They were twins, but they didn't look alike. Esau grew up to be very strong and hairy, while Jacob was a bit small and plain. Esau used to be outside all the time, look-ing after sheep and digging holes. Jacob would sit in his tent all day.

One day Jacob was cooking some soup and Esau came stag-gering up the path. 'I'm starving, is that soup?' he said. Jacob said it was. Then he said, 'I will only give you some if you let me have everything that belongs to Father after he dies.' Well

Esau really was hungry, and the soup looked lovely, so he agreed. 'Promise?' said Jacob, and Esau promised.

A few years later, their father was getting very old and he couldn't see very well. He had always liked Esau a bit more than Jacob, so one day he called Esau and said, 'Go and make me some supper, you know how I like your cooking.' His mother was listening outside the door, and as Esau went out, she called Jacob. Now she liked Jacob better than Esau, so she told him to go and cook some supper for his father.

'He'll think it's Esau,' she said. 'He can't see very well and he might say you can have all the things he owns.'

'No chance,' Jacob replied. 'Esau's all big and hairy, and I'm all small and smooth. If he touches me he will know the difference.'

So do you know what Jacob's mother did?

She stuck some fur to his arms and back, and said, 'That will fool him. You're all hairy now.'

Jacob looked a bit worried, but he thought, 'What have I got to lose?'

The trick worked. Jacob gave his father the supper, got a nice blessing, and hurried out again – just before Esau arrived with his supper.

Esau and his father were so angry, that Jacob thought he'd better leave home. So he did.

His mother told him to visit his uncle Laban, who lived a long way away.

Jacob wasn't all that strong, so he soon fell asleep by the side of the road.

Then he had a wonderful dream. He dreamt that a ladder went all the way from where he was, right into Heaven. And you know what? Walking up and down the ladder were lots and lots of angels. Jacob heard God say that he would look after him, and then he woke up.

'Gosh,' he thought, 'this place must be where you go to Heaven from.' And he put a big stone there to remind him where it was.

Lots of things happened in the next few years. Jacob got married twice. The first girl was a mistake, but in those days people didn't mind if you had more than one wife.

Jacob had been working for his uncle all this time, but one day he decided to leave with his wives and all his sons.

'I miss my brother,' he thought. 'I shall go and see how he is.'

On the way back, Jacob got a bit worried. 'I hope Esau isn't still cross with me,' he said.

But everything was all right. Esau was very pleased to see Jacob again, and welcomed the whole family with open arms.

JOSEPH'S LOVELY COAT

You remember that Jacob had lots of sons? Well, his favourite was Joseph. Joseph was so clever that he could even tell you what dreams are all about. One day he told his brothers he had dreamt that they were all in the field picking corn, and their corn had bowed to his corn. 'That means that one day you'll bow down to me,' he said.

Well, you can imagine how annoyed all his brothers felt about that, but when Jacob suddenly gave his favourite son a special present, that was too much for them. It was a beautiful flowing coat, much smarter than anything the brothers wore, and it was brightly coloured, with lovely patterns.

'This is much nicer than sheepskin,' Joseph said to his brothers.

They were furious. They were so cross they shouted, 'We'll kill you.'

A few days later, Joseph was working in one of the fields, proudly wearing his new coat, when his brothers crept up behind him and jumped on him.

After a struggle, the brothers pulled off Joseph's lovely coat and threw him into a big hole in the ground.

The brothers couldn't decide what to do next, but just at that moment some men passed on their way to Egypt. One of the brothers said, 'Why don't we sell Joseph to those men. How about that?'

So they did, and the men gave them enough pocket money to last at least two weeks.

The brothers were worried about what they could tell their father. 'He'll be mad about this,' one said, 'what can we say?' So do you know what they did? They took Joseph's lovely bright coat, and covered it with stuff that looked like his blood. Then they took the coat to Jacob, and said, 'Oh dear, we think a lion's got our Joseph.'

Jacob cried. He was really cut up about it.

JOSEPH MEETS THE KING
(and helps him)

Joseph had lots of adventures. He worked for a rich man for a long time, and had a row with him for reasons we won't talk about. Then he was put into prison for something he hadn't done, which wasn't very fair.

But, strangely enough, what happened in prison helped him to meet the king.

Locked in with him were two men. One was the King's baker, and the other was his waiter. They were in prison because they had upset the King, probably with their cooking.

These two men both had dreams, and Joseph (you remember that he understood dreams) was able to tell what they meant.

The waiter told his dream first. 'Some grapes suddenly grew on a tree, while I was watching. I picked them and squeezed them into the King's cup. He drank it all up.'

Joseph thought for a minute. 'You're all right there,' he said, 'Pharaoh the King will let you out of prison soon.'

The waiter said, 'Thanks Joseph. That's wonderful.' Well, it was, wasn't it?

Then it was the baker's turn. He hoped his dream would be all right too.

'I was standing with three baskets on my head.' Joseph looked puzzled. The baker continued, 'The top one had lots of cakes and sausage rolls in it for the King. Suddenly, some birds flew down and ate up all the yummies.'

'That's awful,' Joseph said. 'That means you're not going to leave the prison.'

It all came true. The waiter was soon out of prison and back with the King, and the baker had to stay where he was.

Joseph stayed there too, but he wasn't really miserable because he knew that God would look after him.

A few months later, the great King Pharaoh had a dream

that was so awful he nearly fell out of bed, and had to light a candle to cheer himself up.

He had dreamt that he saw seven lovely happy cows, and then seven skinny sad cows following them.

It might not sound a very nasty dream, but Pharaoh was upset.

After a little while he felt better and went back to sleep, but as soon as he turned over he had another dream.

There were seven lovely pieces of corn, all yellow and shiny, and swaying in the sunshine. Then seven nasty small pieces of corn appeared, and the wind blew, and the sky was dark.

That was enough for Pharaoh. He jumped out of bed and walked up and down for the rest of the night.

The next morning Pharaoh was tired and worried. He asked everybody the meaning of his dreams, but everyone said, 'dunno' or 'don't ask me'.

Then the waiter stood up (you remember him from the prison) and said, 'There's a man called Joseph in prison, and he's good at dreams.'

Pharaoh was excited. 'Bring him in,' he commanded.

Soon Joseph was standing in front of the King, without even having a chance to brush his hair.

Pharaoh told him all about the cows and the corn. Joseph said, 'Easy. No problems. Now let me see.' And he thought, and he walked up and down, and he scratched his head and finally shouted, 'I've got it!'

Everybody was excited, and Joseph said, 'The seven fat cows and nice corn mean there's going to be lots of food for seven years. See? And the seven thin cows and mouldy corn means that seven hungry years will follow.'

'That's it!' said Pharaoh, slapping his knee. 'That's it!'

Anyway, to cut a long story short, Joseph was quite right. He became great friends with the King, and was nearly as important.

All the people in the land got lots of food ready in the first seven years, so they had plenty to eat for the bad years.

After a while Joseph's wicked brothers turned up and asked

him for some food, and of course Joseph helped them. It was very nice of him, wasn't it?

Joseph even got old Jacob, his Father, to come and see him.

'Is it really Joseph, my Son?' the old man said. When he said it was, everyone was so happy they cried.

Even God had a little smile to himself.

MOSES – and how he started life

God wasn't completely happy for long. He was very fond of Joseph and his family, and he even liked Pharaoh in a funny way.

But the years passed, and a new King came along who said, 'let's make all the people who aren't Egyptians work for us, because we're Egyptians and they're not.'

Everyone thought they knew what he meant, so it was decided. All the little boys that were born had to go, but the little girls could stay. It was all very unfair.

There was one mother who didn't want her little boy to go, she loved him too much. One day she took him down to the river and put him in a basket, and pushed it away like a boat.

The little boy lay in the basket, watching all the birds, and the clouds, and the trees above him. He was quite happy.

Suddenly, as he was looking up, he saw a big face staring at him. It was the King's daughter.

'Ooh, isn't he sweet,' she said, and she took him home to the Palace.

The little boy's sister saw what happened, and went up to the Princess. 'Shall I find a lady to look after him?' she asked. The princess said yes, and the little girl ran to fetch her mother.

So the little boy was looked after by his own Mummy, and when he was a bit older the Princess showed him to the King, and said, 'Can I keep him Dad? Can I? Can I?' Well, as most fathers do, he said yes, and the princess called him Moses. Wasn't that a nice name?

MOSES . . . . . . later

Moses grew up to be very good indeed. He helped people so much that God decided to have a word with him.

When Moses was looking after his sheep, a bush in front of him burst into flames. Needless to say, Moses was very surprised, and even more so when an angel appeared in it. A voice came from the bush. 'Come here, Moses.' 'Who . . . what . . . umm' said Moses, absolutely amazed.

'Listen,' said God, 'I want you to lead all your people out of Egypt, away from the bad Egyptians and into a wonderful new land.'

God had been watching the people of Moses, who were the children of Israel, and he knew what a horrible time they were having with the bad King. 'Why did you choose me?' asked Moses, 'I'm not very good at that sort of thing.'

God got quite angry, and asked Moses if he trusted him. Moses said that he did, but he didn't think people would listen. God said, 'Your brother Aaron can do all the talking, and you can tell him what to say, and I'll tell you what to say to him.'

Moses was still a bit worried about it, so God showed him how to do all sorts of clever things. 'Throw your walking stick on the ground,' he said. Moses did, and it turned into a snake. 'That's good,' said Moses. Then God turned Moses' hand all white and then pink again, and showed him how to change the colour of water.

Moses said thank you to God, and went to meet his brother. He told Aaron what to say to the children of Israel, and all the time God whispered to Moses, to make sure he knew what to say.

TEN NASTY PLAGUES

Moses wanted to take all his family, the children of Israel, away from Egypt to a land of their own.

He thought he had better ask the King first, so bright and early one morning Moses and Aaron dropped in at the palace.

The Pharaoh (all the Kings were called Pharaoh) said, 'You must be joking. The children of Israel must stay here and work for us. We're far too lazy to do it ourselves.'

Moses whispered to Aaron, and Aaron grumbled at Pharaoh, but it was no good. Even the trick with the walking stick snake didn't impress him.

'Right!' shouted Moses. 'That's it,' shouted Moses. 'Just you wait.' And he stormed out of the palace, waving his fist.

God and Moses had a talk about how mean Pharaoh was, so God stretched to his full height and cried. 'Right!'

Then he came close to Moses, and whispered, 'This is what you do . . .'

God told Moses that the best way to upset Pharaoh was to do lots of nasty things to Egypt. 'A few plagues, eh?' said Moses.

So he went to the river where Pharaoh was, and turned it into blood. Then he did the same with every little river, every lake, every pond. Right down to the last mug of water. Every drop was turned to blood.

'See,' Moses said to Pharaoh. 'Can we leave Egypt now?'

'No!' cried Pharaoh.

'Plague two!' cried Moses.

God left it a week, and then told Moses and Aaron what to do next to worry Pharaoh. 'Wave your magic walking stick,' he said, 'and all the frogs will come out of all the rivers and cover the land.'

Well, that was really horrible for the Egyptians. There were frogs everywhere. In the streets, in the houses, even in people's beds.

Pharaoh ran to Moses and said, 'You can go, you can go. And take your people with you. But please, ask your God to take these frogs away.' (He hated frogs.)

'Fair enough,' said Moses, and he passed the message on to God.

In a little while all the frogs had jumped away.

When Pharaoh saw the last frog leap into the river he said, 'Ha Ha! Fooled you. You try and escape now.'

This time God was really angry. This horrible little Pharaoh had told a lie (and you know how God hates lies) so he said, 'Ah . . . it's time for plague three.'

God made fat lice cover everybody and everything in Egypt, but Pharaoh still said no. So . . . Plague four. God and Moses covered the whole land with flies. The Egyptians could hardly see the sky because the flies came in such enormous clouds.

'Play fair,' Pharaoh said to Moses. 'Why can't your people stay in Egypt, it's not that bad.'

Moses and God said that was no good, so they brought on Plague five, then Plague six, then Plague seven. That reminded God of when he started the world. Rain and hail storms covered the land of Egypt, smashing up the trees, houses, and all the things the people were growing. Then he sent down lots of fires, and still the hail continued.

'That's done it!' cried Pharaoh from his palace. 'They can go away from Egypt, and I hope I never see them again.'

But once again Pharaoh got nasty after the storms had stopped. 'They can't go!' he shouted.

Well, God did another three plagues, just to show who was boss, and finally Pharaoh let the children of Israel leave Egypt. All six hundred thousand of them.

OVER THE RED SEA

You have probably guessed already – Pharaoh changed his mind again. He couldn't help thinking, 'If the children of Israel leave us, who is going to do all the work around here?'

But Moses and all his folk were well on their way out of Egypt. So Pharaoh got all his best horses, all his best men, and all his bright shiny chariots. 'If that doesn't bring them back,' he thought, 'nothing will.'

Now God, as usual, was being a great help to Moses. During the day he sent a lovely cloud to show the way, and at night an enormous flame showed them what was going on.

This was fine for Moses and the children of Israel, but it made it very easy for the Egyptians to find them.

One evening, when they had just got to the beach at the Red Sea, the Egyptians crept up behind them. Luckily God was watching, so he moved the cloud round, and the naughty Egyptians couldn't see Moses.

The Egyptians all stopped their chariots and had a bit of a chat. They decided it was best to bring the children of Israel back to Egypt in the morning. 'Anyway, I'm tired,' said one, yawning. 'We'll sleep here, they can't go very far.'

He was wrong there, because when God's around, anything can happen.

Everyone with Moses was a little worried. 'You said we could get out of Egypt, and now they're chasing us,' they said.

'Don't panic,' Moses said happily, 'God will help us out.'

He was quite right. God told Moses to wave his walking stick over the sea, and they could escape that way.

'It's very deep,' said Moses, 'and I can't swim.'

God told him everything was going to be fine, because the water would actually move out of the way for the children of Israel.

'Move out of the way?' said an astonished Moses. 'Yes,'

said God. 'This will show your people, and those awful Egyptians, just how great I am.'

'It certainly will,' thought Moses.

It happened just as God said. Moses waved his stick, and the sea parted, leaving a dry path right to the other side.

The water was like two enormous walls, one on either side of the path. A few surprised fish had to jump back into the wall, they were afraid of getting dry.

'Come on,' shouted Moses.

All the children of Israel followed him. All their sheep, all their children. Everything they owned. During the night they all got across to the other side of the sea.

But what about those naughty Egyptians?

They woke up the next morning and someone said, 'They've gone!'

'Can't have,' said another. 'What's for breakfast?'

They realised very quickly what had happened. They looked at the Red Sea. They looked at the path. Then they looked at each other. 'Of all the sneaky . . . ' they said.

They jumped into their chariots and in a great cloud of dust rushed down the path. They knew that if they didn't get Moses and his friends back there would be terrible trouble with the Pharaoh.

At that moment the last of the children of Israel scrambled ashore.

All the bad Egyptians were halfway across the Red Sea and God said, 'Moses! wave your stick . . . now!'

He did, and the walls of water crashed down across the path, and all the Egyptians were drowned.

'We're safe!' the children of Israel shouted,

'Hooray!'

And they all had a big dance and a sing song, because they had escaped from Pharaoh, and his dirty jobs, and his horrible Egyptians.

After the party they all fell asleep, and every single one said his prayers, thanking God for getting them out of trouble.

3

BREAD FROM HEAVEN

When Moses and his friends had crossed the Red Sea, they found themselves in a great wilderness. They all began to feel hungry, and just like other children, the children of Israel got a bit miserable when they were hungry. They said things like, 'At least we had enough to eat when we were in Egypt.'

Moses told them not to be so ungrateful, and said that God would look after them. 'You will, won't you?' he said to God afterwards.

'Of course I will,' was the reply. 'Every morning I will send bread from Heaven, and your people can collect it for their families, and eat it.'

'Thanks,' said Moses. 'Will you do that until we're out of the wilderness?'

'Yes,' said God kindly. 'But you must remember, eat it the same day because it goes off. And don't forget about Sunday. You know how I like my Sunday rest, so on Saturday I will send you a different sort of bread. It will last you two days — so don't forget to pick up twice as much.'

God said goodbye, and went back to Heaven.

'Just wait till I tell 'em this,' grinned Moses, 'They'll never believe it!'

The next morning they all got up early and looked round the wilderness.

They thought at first that God had forgotten to send the bread from the sky, but when they looked under the frost on the ground, there it was! Lots and lots of little pieces of bread. They all collected as much as they needed. The people with small families collected a little, and the people with big families collected a lot.

But do you know, some of the children of Israel didn't take any notice of Moses, and tried to keep some bread for the next day. When they looked at it the next morning, it had all gone bad.

God told Moses that he could keep some bread, or Manna as he called it, to show people when they got out of the wilderness, to take with them.

The children of Israel collected fresh bread every morning while they were in the wilderness. But they never collected it on Sundays, because they knew God was staying in bed late, so they did the same.

THE CHILDREN MEET GOD

Well, the children of Israel ran out of water and they grumbled. They had a battle with some people and they grumbled.

In fact they sometimes grumbled so much that God wondered why he helped them at all.

Finally he decided he should meet them, for none of the Israelites, apart from Moses, had even spoken to God.

At the time they were all by a big mountain called Mount Sinai. God said to Moses, 'In three days time, bring the children of Israel near the mountain, and I will speak to them. Now if they believe me and trust me after that, I will make them very holy.'

'Good idea,' said Moses. 'I'll tell them right away.'

Three days later, the people all stood in the rain waiting to see God.

Suddenly an enormous cloud appeared and hovered over the mountain. There was lightning, and thunder, and the sound of trumpets getting louder and louder.

The Israelites looked at the mountain, and looked at each other, biting their nails.

Moses shouted, 'Are you there?'

'I am,' God thundered.

The children of Israel all stared in wonder. God was real, and they could see him, and they could hear him.

They thought it was wonderful.

THE TEN DO'S AND DON'TS

Moses walked through the mighty storm, up the mountain towards God.

The children of Israel watched the lone figure staggering into the blackness, as the thunder and lightning raged.

God said, 'I am your God, come to me.'

Moses got to the top, and God told him ten things to remember. They were the ten things that make a good or bad person. They were called The Commandments.

'The first thing to remember
When you are being good
Is have no other gods but me
I don't see why you should.
The second thing is simple.
Whatever else you do
Don't worship models made of clay
Don't make an idol in that way
I'd get annoyed with you.

And in the third commandment
You mustn't ever say
God, Lord or Heaven in a joke
For that would spoil my day.
The fourth thing you must never do —
Upset my Sunday rest.
I've given you the other days
To do your work in many ways
On Sunday you can have a laze
And wear your Sunday best.

Number five's a good one,
Remember what I say,
Don't ever upset Mum and Dad
In any little way.

The sixth commandment sure makes sense
I know that when I say
No killing is allowed, but then
You wouldn't would you? Even when
You get annoyed with other men
And don't get your own way.

If you are getting married
The seventh rule is this,
Don't try and love another
Or give the girls a kiss.
At number eight there's something
I'm sure you'd never do,
Don't steal a thing, at any time
From anyone, for any rhyme
Or reason – as it is a crime,
And they would capture you.

The ninth one to remember
If you do as you're bid,
Don't blame a man for stealing
Unless you're sure he did.
With all the people in the world
Your neighbour is a friend.
So don't be jealous even when
You want his goat or horse or hen,
For that's commandment number ten,
It's at the very end.

Moses listened open mouthed as God told him all about the commandments. 'Can you say it again? I didn't have time to write them down.'

God said nothing, but waved his mighty hand over Mount Sinai. Lightning flashed, and smoke covered Moses. When it cleared, he saw all the commandments beautifully written on two pieces of stone.

Moses thanked God for his help, and began to stagger down the mountain with his commandments.

On the way down he had a good think about things.

THE BABY COW — MADE OF GOLD

Meanwhile, the people were getting edgy. They hadn't seen Moses for ages, and they wanted to do something.

'Make us something to say our prayers to, Aaron,' one of them said. 'Yes, come on Aaron.' The crowd got excited.

'Tell you what I'll do,' Aaron answered. 'Take off your gold rings and earrings.'

They all looked over his shoulder as Aaron started dropping the gold into a pot. They were worried as he lit a fire under the pot and the gold began to melt. 'What's he doing?' they whispered. 'Wait and see,' hissed Aaron, stirring briskly.

Soon the gold was all in one lump, and Aaron got to work. He made a calf out of the gold.

'A golden calf!' said the excited people. 'Aaron, you're the greatest!'

'Well, thank you. It was nothing,' Aaron replied, modestly.

You see, in the second commandment, God had said that if anybody made a model of something, and then prayed to it, they would be in trouble. This was just what the naughty Israelites did. And as for Aaron, he should have known better.

Just at the height of the excitement, when everyone was dancing round the golden calf, and singing their heads off, Moses reached the bottom of the mountain.

'Now what are you doing?' he yelled. 'Can't I leave you for five minutes?' And he was so angry that he threw his commandments on the ground and they smashed to pieces.

The singing stopped, and everyone silently looked at Moses.

'What's wrong, Moses?' they asked.

'You can't do this!' he shouted. 'Making models, praying and singing. It's not allowed!'

And he ran up to the golden calf and threw it in the fire, and he threw all the bits into the water and made the Israelites drink it.

Boy, was he angry.

Some time later, Moses began to feel sorry that he had broken the commandments, especially after God had taken so much trouble making them.

So he carved some blocks of stone in the shape he remembered, and God wrote exactly the same words on them.

'Thank goodness,' thought Moses, 'God remembered every single one.'

MOSES GOES TO HEAVEN

Finally Moses and the children of Israel reached another wilderness very close to the land that God had promised them.

The Israelites still grumbled. Moses couldn't seem to do anything right. The people thought it was his fault that there was nothing to eat but Manna (the bread from Heaven). They thought it was his fault that the birds God sent them didn't taste very nice, or they ate too many of them, and they were sick. They even blamed Moses when they found out that the people in the promised land were bigger that they were.

'If we have to fight them to get our land, we'll never win!' they cried. 'They're far too big. They'll kill us all. We're finished. Oh why aren't we back in Egypt?'

Moses tried to stop them getting upset. 'Oh for heaven's sake, be quiet. I'm doing my best.' And he was.

With God's help, the Israelites did beat some of the people. Of course, they thought they had done it by themselves, but it was really God's work.

Throughout the years God had got more and more displeased with the children of Israel. He had heard them grumble all the time, and they didn't very often thank him for anything.

One day he said to Moses, 'Your people can never live in the land I promised them. I will save Canaan for their children, perhaps they'll appreciate it.'

Moses tried to persuade God to change his mind, but God was determined.

'You are my special person, Moses,' he said. 'And the people haven't really listened to you much.'

'I know,' said Moses, looking sad.

The children of Israel wandered in the wilderness for forty years. They had lots of their own children by then, and God was ready to send them into Canaan.

One of the young boys came to Moses and said, 'Are you

ready Moses? We're crossing the river to our land today.'

Moses looked very old and tired as he spoke to the boy. 'I won't be coming with you, God needs me in Heaven soon. Go and get everyone, I want to talk to them.'

All the people came to Moses and he told them to obey God's commandments. They would have to love the people they lived and worked with, and they shouldn't steal or kill because God wouldn't like it.

Moses held out his hands so the people could help him up. 'I shall go to the top of that hill, and look at the promised land. Goodbye, all of you.'

The children of Israel sadly looked at the old man as he climbed up the hill to have a last look at Canaan, before he went to be with God.

THE WALLS OF JERICHO FALL DOWN

God chose Joshua to take over from Moses. The Israelites needed someone to lead them, and Joshua was just the man.

He sent two men into the town of Jericho, in Canaan, to see what it was like. When they got there they stayed with a lady called Rahab. She told them that the King knew they were in town, and that he'd heard about the Israelites and God, and was very worried.

'Hide on the roof,' she told them. 'The guards will be here soon.'

The two men looked at each other, and climbed on to the roof as quickly as possible.

The guards searched every house in the town, but they couldn't find the two Israelites. Meanwhile the two men left Rahab's house, and hid in the mountains for a few days. Before they left, they told the kind lady that when the Israelites attacked the town of Jericho, she and her family would be safe. Joshua and God would see to that.

Finally the two men got back to their friends. 'We're laughing,' they said. 'The people of Jericho are terrified of us.'

'Are you sure?' asked Joshua.

'Of course,' they answered. 'No problems.'

Joshua had a chat with God, and told him about the high walls all round Jericho. 'They're enormous,' he cried, pointing his finger straight up in the air. 'We'll never climb them. So how are we going to take over the town, and drive out all the people? We've had enough of living in tents, we want houses. How can we get them with those great walls in the way?'

'Ummmm . . . ' said God, scratching his head, 'that's tricky.' He sat for a long time thinking about it, and Joshua was just about to suggest that they shouldn't bother, when God said, 'I've got it!'

Joshua said, 'Go on . . . ' and after God had whispered the idea to him, Joshua clicked his heels in the air and happily returned to his people.

45

Joshua made seven of his best priests walk round the walls of Jericho blowing trumpets. He told the people to follow, but warned them to be very quiet.

Several Jerichoites looked over the walls in amazement, as the Israelites walked round the town blowing trumpets.

The next morning Joshua and his friends got up very early and did exactly the same thing. By this time everyone in the town was talking about it. They were saying things like, 'They're going mad. They must be eating too much Manna,' and, 'Their God's let them down this time.'

Joshua led his trumpeters, soldiers, and people round the walls of Jericho for the third (and last) time.

They surrounded the whole town, and when Joshua gave the signal, the trumpets sounded, and the people shouted, yelled, and stamped their feet. There was such a terrible noise that the walls of Jericho cracked, crumbled and finally fell like a pile of toy bricks.

The Israelites ran over the rubble to attack the amazed Jerichoites.

They won the battle, and took over the town. The only people who were safe were the nice lady and her family.

So the Israelites were in the promised land at last. That night Joshua made sure they said a very special thank you to their real leader. That's right . . . God.

GIDEON HAS A DATE
WITH AN ANGEL

As you may have noticed, there was always one man whom God treated as a very special person. Moses was one, and Joshua was another.

Quite a few years later, God started watching a man called Gideon. He was a good man, always helpful and polite. His mother only had to say, 'Can you help with the washing up,' and he was there.

The Israelites had had their troubles in the promised land.

They still grumbled a bit, and God still had to punish them sometimes.

When Gideon had grown up, the children of Israel had just had a few years of punishment. They had been beaten in battles, they had been hungry, and some had lost their homes.

God decided it was time to change all that. One day he sent an angel to Gideon, while he was working in the field. Gideon didn't know the angel was there, in fact he would probably have carried on digging all day, if the angel hadn't said, 'God is with you, you know.'

Gideon looked up and said, 'Who . . . what?' and various other surprised things.

'Don't be afraid,' said the angel. 'I won't hurt you.'

They had a long talk. Gideon asked the angel why God was making things so difficult if he was really with them. 'There's the Midianites,' he said, 'they're being horrible to us, and I'm a bit worried about those Amalekites.'

The angel told Gideon to lead his people into battle, and said that he was bound to win.

Gideon went out the next day and got all his people together. They really got those baddies on the run.

God was so pleased that he made sure everything went well for the Israelites for the next forty years.

But, you've guessed it. The children of Israel soon upset God again.

SAMSON TRIES TO MAKE A JOKE

A nasty crowd called the Philistines had won a lot of battles against the Israelites and were running the country. God made sure this happened because the people of Israel had upset him again with their selfishness and evil ways.

After a very long time God decided to make a man who would be strong enough to beat the Philistines.

So Samson was born. When he was still very young, God told his parents that they should never cut Samson's hair. The parents didn't understand why, but they agreed.

Samson grew up to be very long haired (he never had a haircut), handsome and very, very strong. He was so strong that he could lift people with one hand.

Now it so happened that he loved a girl from the Philistines. Of course his parents weren't very happy about this, they wanted him to marry an Israelite.

Samson was determined to marry the girl, so finally his parents gave their blessing.

On the way to see his girlfriend he was walking through some trees, and a great lion jumped on him. There was a struggle, and Samson killed the lion with his bare hands. The fight took so long that Samson was very late, so he hurried away to the Philistine girl's house.

A few days later he passed the dead lion, and inside was a swarm of bees, and lots of honey.

Samson took out some of the yummy honey and ate it. When he had licked the last sticky finger, he returned home.

On the day of the wedding everyone had a lot of wine, and Samson stood up and said, 'Listen, you Philistines. I've got a riddle for you. Ready?' They all filled up their mugs again and said they were.

> 'Meat came out of the eater.
> Sweetness came out of the strong.'

Samson looked round at the blank faces. 'All right?' he asked, 'do you understand it?' He poured himself another mug of wine, grinned, and slumped back in his chair.

Now, as everyone should know, no one makes a fool of a Philistine. They just don't think it's funny. The ones at the wedding feast were no exception. They were furious about Samson's riddle. 'I don't get it,' one said. 'It's not very clever anyway,' said another.

In fact they got so annoyed that they told Samson's wife to find out the answer, or they would burn her house down.

That wasn't very nice, was it?

His wife asked Samson the answer to the riddle and he wouldn't tell her, so she burst into tears and cried for seven whole days.

Samson got so fed up with it, that he finally told her the answer; she told the men, and they told Samson.

'A lion with a bees' nest in it.'

(If you don't understand the riddle, don't worry too much – it wasn't a very good one.)

Samson was furious. 'You told them!' he yelled at his wife. 'I can't stand you any longer, crying all the time, and letting me down in front of the Philistines.'

Samson stormed out of the house and went back to live with his Mother and Father.

SAMSON HAS A HAIRCUT

Samson spent a lot of his time doing as much as he could to annoy the Philistines. He burnt their corn, ruined their olive trees and even had fights with them. One day he got an old bone and killed over a thousand men by himself.

As you can see, God had made Samson the strongest man in the whole world, and this began to worry the Philistines more and more.

Samson didn't see his wife again. He decided he loved a girl called Delilah.

Now Samson, for all his strength and good looks, wasn't very good at choosing women. Delilah was no exception. She was pretty enough (well Samson thought so) but she was bad right through, like an old apple.

When the Philistines said to her, 'Come on Del, why is Samson so strong?' she said, 'Give me some silver, and I'll find out for you.'

Samson and Delilah were sitting together one day, talking about nothing in particular, when the bad lady said, 'Ooh Sam, you are strong.' Samson gave one of his half smiles and said, 'I know.'

Delilah asked him what the secret of his strength was, and he made up a story about being tied up in willow branches. 'That,' he said, 'would make me a weakling immediately.'

Delilah told the Philistines about this, and the next day they hid in her room while she tied him up in willow branches.

As we all know it was really Samson's long hair that made him strong, so when Delilah cried, 'The Philistines are here!' Samson jumped up, pulled off the branches as if they were pieces of paper, and threw out the Philistines.

Delilah tried a few more times to find out the secret of Samson's strength, but each time he made up a different silly story.

Finally he told her the truth.

'It's my hair. If it is ever cut I go weak, just like the skinny Philistines.'

So when Samson was asleep, Delilah and the Philistines cut his hair.

When he woke up he felt all floppy, and he could hardly stand up, let alone fight the Philistines.

'Got you at last!' they cried. 'This will teach you to burn our corn, pinch our olives and fight our men.'

They tied him up, and dragged the helpless Samson away.

SAMSON BRINGS THE HOUSE DOWN

The Philistines made sure that Samson couldn't see, and made him work hard in prison.

He worked from early morning until late at night, pushing a giant wheel to make flour for the Philistines' bread. It was the sort of job that donkeys usually do.

Samson was really sad. His girlfriend had let him down, his strength was gone, he couldn't see properly, and his job didn't seem to have any future.

'Please God,' he would say, 'why have you forgotten me? I did my best for you.'

But he never got an answer.

One day all the Philistines in the land had got together in a big house to worship their own god. They didn't believe in Samson's God, but by the end of that day they would probably have changed their minds.

The crowd decided it was time to have a laugh at Samson.

'Bring him out of prison,' they shouted, 'let's see how the great strong man is getting on.'

Samson was brought from the prison, and his guards put him between two mighty pillars in the house. The Philistines laughed at him, teased him, and threw things at him.

'Look at the strong man now!' they yelled. 'Isn't your God going to help you?'

Samson listened to the cruel Philistines, and whispered to God, 'Now my hair has grown again, can you make me strong just once more?'

He pleaded with God, and finally he felt strength coming back into his body.

He reached out to touch the two great pillars of the house, and using every bit of strength he could muster, pushed against them. He was just beginning to think it wouldn't work, when . . . yes! The pillars moved a bit! Samson gave a final mighty

54

push and the pillars cracked, and smashed, bringing the great building crumbling to the ground.

'Thank you God,' he cried, and Samson died, taking with him every man in the building.

His life's work was done, he had got revenge on the evil Philistines, and Samson happily joined his God in Heaven.

DAVID AND GOLIATH

Many, many years later, the horrible Philistines were still in the land of the Israelites. Saul was the leader of Israel's army and he was their King.

One day Saul was feeling really bad tempered, he was shouting at everyone and grumbling.

One of his servants came into his room and said, 'I know a boy who will cheer you up. He plays the harp, and you know how you like harp music.'

'He'd better be good, or else . . . ' Saul didn't have to finish his sentence, the servant hurried out of the room. He ran to Jesse's house a few streets away.

'King Saul wants to hear David play the harp,' he said to Jesse.

Jesse's son David was soon with Saul, playing the harp and trying to cheer up the miserable King.

It worked. Saul soon started tapping his feet and smiling.

David often played for Saul after that, and they became great friends.

In the meantime, the Philistines were on a hill not far from the army of the Israelites.

The Philistines were all dressed in freshly polished armour, and were sure they would win, because they had one soldier who was a real giant. He was nearly twice as big as an ordinary man, and strong with it. His name was Goliath.

The army of Israel came towards them and waited nervously to see what would happen. Saul joined them and said, 'What are we waiting for?'

The soldiers pointed out what they were waiting for. 'We would feel happier if HE wasn't there.' Saul looked at the mighty Goliath, and Goliath looked at Saul, and Saul looked at the white worried soldiers behind him.

Goliath spoke first. 'You measly Israelites. I could beat any one of you. Want to try me, hey, hey?'

Saul turned to his men, hoping for someone to offer to fight the giant Goliath.

No one put their hand up.

David was looking after his sheep when his father said, 'Here you are son, take this cheese to your brothers in the army.'

David wasn't big enough to be a soldier. He was only a lad, but he was strong, handsome, and very good.

'Yes, Dad,' he said, being eager to help his parent (as good boys do), 'I'll leave right away.'

When he reached the army camp he realised everyone was rather quiet. Just at that moment Goliath started shouting again. 'Come on, send out your strongest man. If he wins the fight we will be your servants. If I win the fight you'll still be our servants.'

Saul looked at his men, hoping more and more that someone would fight the loud-mouthed Goliath.

'Come on lads,' Saul pleaded.

David came up to Saul and said, 'How can he win when we have God on our side? God will help me to beat this awful man. Besides, the bigger they are, the harder they fall.'

Saul looked at little David, then he looked at big Goliath, and then he looked at little David again. 'You? . . . against him? Do you realise what you're saying, boy?'

Saul thought for a minute, and decided that David should have a go. After all, nobody else wanted to.

Saul and David's brothers stood the boy on a rock, and proceeded to dress him in armour. When he was ready he tried to walk and fell over, so he stood up and fell over again. 'This is no good,' a hollow voice came from inside the armour. 'The suit is too big.'

'We haven't got any smaller ones,' said Saul.

After a lot of discussion, David decided he didn't want armour, helmet or weapons. 'I've got my little sling,' he said sheepishly.

'A sling? Against . . . thing?' said Saul, not realising it had rhymed.

David picked up some shiny pebbles, and began to walk towards the mighty Goliath.

Goliath smiled, and then he laughed and he laughed some

more. 'Look at the size of him! Is that the best you can do?'

Goliath got out his great sword, and was just about to slice little David in half, when David whirled round his sling and a stone hit Goliath right on the head.

The once mighty giant fell, and the ground shook for miles around.

David was carried high on the shoulders of the Israelites. 'We've won,' he cried. 'With God's help we have beaten the Philistines!'

That story shows you that you don't have to be strong to win in life, and you don't have to be taller than everyone else to succeed.

With a keen mind and a lot of faith (that's what David had) you can be a winner every time.

SOLOMON – HIS WISDOM AND HIS GOLD

Many things happened in the next few years, far too many to go into. David married Saul's daughter. David became King. David became an old man.

We will take up the story just after old David died, leaving his young son Solomon as King.

Solomon was very young, and didn't know much about anything, as he was little more than a schoolboy. One night he spoke to God in a dream. 'My Lord, you have put me in charge of a wonderful country, and there are so many clever people in it, that I feel quite dumb at times.'

God was always very understanding to the people he chose, so he said, 'What do you want most of all in the whole world?'

Now a lot of young people would have asked for money, or a nice fast chariot to drive, or as much gold as they could carry, but Solomon was different. All he said was, 'Please God, give me the wisdom and kindness to make me a great King to my people.'

God was really pleased about that.

'Solomon,' he said, 'you will be the wisest King in the world. You will know more than even your father David did.'

'Thank you,' said Solomon, and he woke up from his dream.

Things turned out just as God said. Solomon became the wisest man in the world, and if people asked him anything at all, he could answer them. Some people wanted to know how to do things and he would tell them. Other people wanted to know where things were, or how far it was, or who did it, or why it happened, and he told them.

Solomon knew everything.

As a special thank you to God, Solomon decided to build a wonderful temple to pray in.

'We'll have gold everywhere,' he told the builders. 'We'll have gold floors, gold walls, gold vases, gold doors, gold everything!'

Solomon was excited. 'We'll have gold seats, gold lamps, gold altar. We'll even have a couple of gold angels on the roof!'

Solomon rubbed his hands together and dashed off to arrange things.

God watched as the wonderful temple was built. He was pleased that Solomon was doing it for him, but he thought all the gold was a bit unnecessary. After all, you can pray to God from anywhere. It doesn't have to be made of gold, does it?

All the parts of the temple were made far away, so that the noise of the hammers and chisels wouldn't disturb the holy place.

Then the pieces were all put together quietly, and sure enough, seven years later, the temple was ready. Solomon put the finishing touch to it by placing the two stones with the ten commandments on them, near the altar.

All the holiest of the holy men of Israel came round that day, and the temple was so full of holiness that they didn't dare say a word.

Solomon blessed the temple and the people, and said, 'This place is built to say thank you to God, for helping Moses get the children of Israel out of Egypt, and into this wonderful land.'

Solomon was standing at the window of his house one day, when he saw a crowd of people coming down the road. There were elephants, camels, and servants carrying gifts. Right in the middle was a very special elephant with a sort of bed on its back. Lying on this bed was a beautiful woman. It was the Queen of Sheba.

Solomon ran out to meet her. She slid gracefully down the side of the elephant, and shook the excited King by the hand.

'I have heard how clever you are,' she said, 'so I thought I would come and ask you some questions.'

Solomon nodded. 'Try me.'

'How far is it to Sheba?' she asked. Solomon thought for a minute, and gave her the right answer. She asked him lots of other questions too, like what was the length of the river Nile, and how many people lived in Jerusalem. 'Right again!' she said after a while, 'Really Solomon, you do know everything! I thought I would catch you out, but I can't.'

The Queen of Sheba gave the wise King lots of spice, precious stones, and lots more gold. Then she returned to her own home, feeling happy that their countries were friendly.

After the Queen left, Solomon had a very successful year. He was given so much gold that he became the richest man in the world, as well as the wisest.

Now unfortunately Solomon began thinking too much about his gold and not enough about his God. That was his big mistake. Solomon started making everything out of gold. Every cup, dish and bowl in his house was gold, and even his throne was made of ivory and gold. There were gold lions next to the throne, and he had some steps built up to the throne with – you've guessed it – gold lions on each step.

Meanwhile God was feeling sad. Solomon hadn't been as good a King as David, and wasn't nearly as holy. So one day Solomon had to leave all his golden goodies and join God in Heaven.

Somebody should have told Solomon that a much better way of being happy was to be a little less greedy, and think about God a bit more. After all – however much gold you have, you can't take it with you when you go.

ELIJAH

Solomon may have been very clever, but he certainly wasn't bright enough to keep the country of Israel together. The land was separated – the north was still Israel, but the south was Judah. After about fifty years a King came along called Ahab. He didn't believe in the proper God, and preferred to pray to a pretend god – Baal.

Elijah was God's chosen man at that time, and one day he said to King Ahab, 'Since you don't believe in God, there will be no rain in this land unless I say so. See?'

Ahab was understandably furious, so Elijah thought he'd better run away and hide in the mountains by a stream. Every day God sent ravens to feed him. They brought bread and meat, and he drank the water from the stream.

Finally the stream dried up, obviously because there hadn't been any rain.

Elijah thought, 'I won't make it rain yet. It's too soon.' So he stayed in hiding, in various places, until one day God said to him, 'Go to Ahab, and show him just how useless his god is.'

Elijah thought for a moment. 'How can I do that?'

God came very close to Elijah and whispered in his ear, 'This is what you do . . . '

Elijah walked boldly into the King's palace and commanded Ahab to collect all his priests, and send them to Mount Carmel.

Ahab said he would. He was really very worried about the water shortage, and thought that obeying Elijah was probably the best thing to do. After all, Elijah was the only one who could make it rain.

They all got together on Mount Carmel. There was Elijah, all the priests, and a very worried King Ahab. 'What are you going to do?' he asked. 'Wait and see,' was the reply.

The priests were instructed to get some meat, build a fire round it, but not to light it.

'Now,' said Elijah, 'get your god to light that. Bet you can't.'

5

The priests started making moaning noises, and waving their arms about.

Nothing happened.

They cried louder and louder, and even cut their fingers to see if that would work. But nothing happened. The fire looked as cold as ever, and the meat still looked raw.

King Ahab started hopping from one foot to the other, and looking at his finger nails as if he didn't really care anyway.

The priests shouted louder, and did strange dances round the fire.

Elijah smiled. 'Perhaps he's gone out for the day. Perhaps your god is asleep.'

The priests glared at him, and finally when it was getting dark, they said, 'All right. You do it then.'

Just to make it seem even more clever, Elijah poured water all over his fire.

'Your God will never light that!' King Ahab laughed.

Elijah didn't say a word. He looked up to Heaven, said a prayer, and a mighty flash of fire appeared and burnt everything.

All the people were amazed. 'Elijah, your God is the real God and the only God,' they said.

Elijah smiled. 'That's right.'

Later that evening the rain started, and all the people were happy again.

Which all goes to prove, you must have . . . that's right, faith.

ELIJAH GOES, ELISHA ARRIVES

King Ahab's wife got very upset about Elijah, and all the fuss he had caused. 'Just wait till I get my hands on him,' she cried.

Once again Elijah thought it was time to run and hide for a while, so he went to stay in the wilderness. While he was there, God made sure he had enough to eat. An angel brought him some cake and a jar of water.

One night, while Elijah slept under the stars, an angel came down and whispered to him. He heard the still small voice tell him to travel to Damascus and find a man called Elisha. He would follow in Elijah's footsteps.

Old Elijah woke up and tried to remember the name. 'It sounds very like mine,' he thought, 'Elijah, Elisha – I won't forget that.'

He found Elisha, and they stayed together for a long time. Elisha learned everything from Elijah. All about God, all about being good, and all about helping people.

Finally old Elijah realised it was time for him to join God in Heaven.

He turned to Elisha and said, 'Bring fifty of our followers, and come with me. They must see the way God collects me, and they will trust you.'

All the people lined up by the river Jordan, and waited.

Suddenly in the sky, they could see a flaming object approaching. As it got nearer they realised it was a chariot and two horses of fire.

Elijah stepped into it, and as the chariot flew into the air, the old man dropped his cloak for Elisha.

As he put on the cloak Elisha said, 'Please God, give me the same powers and spirit as Elijah.'

And that is what he got. His followers joined him, and they all said a prayer to God.

Elisha did lots of wonderful things. One day a man named

Naaman sent him a note, saying he had a disease which made his skin white. Elisha decided to see him, and Naaman arrived.

Elisha thought for a moment. 'Simple!' he said, 'Go and wash seven times in the River Jordan, and you'll be cured.'

Naaman said, 'How can that cure me? Why can't I wash in a river nearer home? I don't understand.'

Somebody whispered to him that it was better to do as Elisha told him, because Elisha was always right.

The man bathed seven times in the River Jordan, and his skin was no longer white, but just as pinky as a baby's. 'How can I repay you?' he said to Elisha. 'Here, take some gold, take some silver. Take some clothes.'

Elisha told the man that it was God's work, and he certainly didn't need the money.

Naaman thanked Elisha again, and began to drive home in his chariot.

Now there was a bad servant who worked for Elisha, and when he overheard all this he thought, 'Well, if they don't need any gold, I certainly do.'

He ran after Naaman and said, 'Elisha's changed his mind. Give me the gold.'

The man did so, and the servant returned to Elisha's home.

'Where have you been?' enquired Elisha. 'Oh . . . um . . . nowhere,' the servant stuttered.

Elisha knew where he had been, and he was very angry.

'Try and take gold for God's work, would you?' he shouted. 'As a punishment, you can have the disease the other man was cured of.'

Elisha pointed his finger, and the servant left the house. He was as white as snow.

Many years later the old Elisha realised it was time to go time. He blessed his country, prayed for their peace, and went to join his friend Elijah in Heaven.

BOOKS, BATTLES AND BURN-UPS

After Elisha died a lot of other men followed in his footsteps, showing everyone the power of God. These men knew that the people of Israel would soon be split up. There was a big city in Israel, Samaria, that was captured by the Assyrians, who made the Israelites run all over the place and finally settle in many different countries.

However, the town that everybody wanted to get at was Jerusalem, but God wouldn't have that. 'Just let them try,' he said.

Many years later a book was found, that contained lots of rules, and told everyone how to behave towards God.

Josiah, who was King in Jerusalem at the time, was shown the book. He read it from end to end (he couldn't put it down), and then told his people to read it and understand it.

Some of the people had made models of rams and horses, and lots of other things that they said prayers to. Josiah stopped all that. He burnt all the models, and showed all the men and women of Jerusalem that a much better way was to pray to God, and follow the words of the book.

Josiah was a very holy King. He turned to God for help in everything, and God was very pleased with him.

After Josiah went to Heaven everyone forgot about the book and carried on fighting, and the Assyrians were beaten by the people of Babylon. One of Josiah's followers, Jeremiah, thought this was bad news. He knew it wouldn't be long before Jerusalem was beaten.

Jeremiah told quite a few people what he thought, and finally upset them so much that they imprisoned him in a muddy hole in the ground. His followers helped him escape by pulling him out with some sheets tied together, but he was soon back in prison again.

All this story is far too long to go into, you would soon stop listening if you heard every detail. Jerusalem was beaten, because God was no longer pleased with the people. They were captured by the Babylonians and kept in Babylon.

These Israelites had a sad time, being ordered around by Nebuchadnezzar (we'll call him Neb) who was the King of Babylon.

He was a bad man who didn't think of God, he only thought of himself. Now some people are conceited, but King Neb must have taken the biscuit.

He thought he was so great that he had a statue of himself made. It was about twice as high as a house, and was carved completely in gold.

When the statue was finished he was so pleased with it that he told everyone to come and see it.

'When the music stops,' he shouted, 'you must all get on your knees and pray to my statue. If you don't you will certainly be thrown into a fiery furnace.'

Nobody liked the idea of being thrown into a fiery furnace, so they all did as King Neb said.

All except three men of Israel. You probably know why they didn't want to – they believed in God, and didn't want to hurt his feelings.

God looked down from Heaven and decided to look after these three men.

Shadrach, Meshach and Abednego, for those were their names, bravely faced the angry King.

'Why didn't you pray to my new gold statue?' he shouted, marching up and down the room.

'It's not for real,' they said. 'Only our God's for real.'

King Neb's eyes looked as fiery as the furnace as he cried, 'Burn them!'

The guards grabbed the three men, and marched them off to the furnace. The guards made the fire seven times hotter than usual, to make sure it would work. It was so hot that some of the King's men had to go back, in case they got burnt.

Shadrach, Meshach and Abednego were tied up and thrown into the fire. The guards couldn't believe their eyes, for the flames were licking all round the men, but they weren't burnt.

They just stood in the furnace, smiling happily, without burning themselves or the clothes they were wearing.

When King Neb saw this he was absolutely amazed (wouldn't you be?). He said, 'Your God must be the real God, and you are the servants of God.'

He walked away scratching his head.

That day he told his people to believe in the real and only God, and anyone who didn't believe, or said anything against God, would be punished.

And what about Shadrach, Meshach and Abednego? They were set free, and King Neb made sure they all got good jobs in Babylon.

DANIEL READS THE WRITING ON THE WALL

King Nebuchadnezzar always believed in God after the fiery furnace business. A few years later he went to Heaven, leaving his son, the evil Belshazzar, to be King.

Belshazzar didn't care about anything. He had no faith in God, and spent his time drinking wine with all the ladies, and having big dinner parties. He even drank wine from holy glasses, which made God so angry that he finally decided it was time to do something about this wicked man.

One night when Belshazzar had a few friends in, and was drinking a great deal of wine, a mysterious hand appeared and started writing on the wall of his room. Belshazzar leapt to his feet, knocking over all the wine, and cried, 'Look!' His knees started knocking together, as the strange words formed on the brickwork.

'Mene, mene, tekel, Upharsin,' it read.

'Mene, mene, tekel, Upharsin?' Belshazzar mumbled, 'What on earth does that mean?'

He sent for all the land's cleverest men, imploring them to solve the mystery.

'What does it mean?' he said sadly. 'All this business is quite putting me off my wine, and I haven't smiled for a week.'

He paced up and down. He tried reading the words backwards and that didn't work. He tried putting the first letter at the end, and that didn't work. The more he looked at the writing on the wall, the more it didn't make sense.

One of the ladies of the house was so worried about the miserable King that she went to him, and recommended a man who was brought from Jerusalem when King Neb was alive. 'His name is Daniel,' she said. 'He is one of the cleverest men in the country. Just you wait and see.'

Soon Daniel was standing in front of the evil King. He took one look at the wall and said, 'You have been a bad man,

Belshazzar. You have got drunk and misbehaved, and you never loved the real God. All you have loved is gold, silver, and any gods that you think will let you have a nice time. It's all too bad of you, Belshazzar.'

The King looked very ashamed. He promised Daniel to make him the third most important man in the country if he knew the meaning of the writing on the wall.

'Right,' said Daniel. 'It means that God has judged your country and you. He thinks you are both no good, so He is going to divide the country into two.'

Belshazzar was really upset. Soon after Daniel left the room the King was killed, and no one was sure if he went to Heaven or not; but they didn't think so, because you're meant to have faith. That's the only way to get to Heaven — but you know that by now, don't you?

DANIEL AND THE LIONS

Belshazzar's place as King was taken by Darius. He was a good man, and great friends with Daniel.

Darius organised things so that lots of princes and presidents ruled different parts of his Kingdom. He put Daniel in charge of these men, which didn't please the princes and presidents at all. So of course they decided to spoil things for Daniel, hoping that the King would chuck him out. They watched Daniel continuously, hoping that he would be unfaithful to the King, or make a mistake in running things. Daniel handled everything perfectly, he was absolutely faultless.

After a few weeks, the bad princes and presidents got together to try and decide what to do. 'Let's tell the King that Daniel's not really doing his job properly,' said one. 'That wouldn't work,' said another, 'the King knows Daniel's working well. There's only one way to handle this.' He beckoned the others to come closer. 'Let's tell King Darius to sign a paper saying that no one is allowed to ask anything of any god for a month, they can only ask the King.'

They all giggled at this, and slapped each other on the back, and crept away to write the letter.

King Darius was sitting on his throne when the little group of princes and presidents came in.

'Oh mighty King, oh fine King, oh great King – live for ever,' they cried. King Darius asked them to get on with it, and they showed him the paper and asked him to sign it. Darius was pleased that they had thought of him, and didn't suppose for a minute that they were really doing all this to get at Daniel.

At the bottom of the letter it said that anybody who prayed to any god would be thrown into a den of lions. King Darius winced at the thought of it, but signed his royal name at the bottom.

It all worked just as the evil men planned.

Pretty soon Daniel was found praying to God (as he did every night) and was hauled in front of King Darius.

Although he didn't want to do it, the King had to keep his word, so Daniel had to go to the den of nasty lions.

As Daniel was leaving the room, the King whispered, 'Your God will look after you, won't he?' Daniel winked as the soldiers marched him away.

That night the King couldn't sleep at all. He paced up and down, and wouldn't eat or listen to music. The next morning he got up very early and hurried down to the lions' den.

There was Daniel, and he was perfectly all right. The King breathed a sigh of relief as he watched the docile lions licking Daniel's nose, resting their heads on his knee, and letting him pat them.

The King was delighted. He insisted that Daniel should be brought out of the lions' den, and returned to the palace.

'Your God is certainly the real God,' he said to Daniel. 'What other god could command lions like that?'

He spread the word to all his people about Daniel's God, telling them to worship him forever.

And what about the evil princes and presidents? We won't go into what happened to them, but you can be sure it had something to do with the lions.

THE RETURN TO JERUSALEM

The people of Israel were called the Jews. With the attack of the city of Jerusalem they spread all over the country, some hiding, some setting up home in a different town, some the prisoners of the Babylonians.

Many of these good people had a feeling that one day they would go back to their homes in Jerusalem, and they were quite right. God made King Darius want to help the Jews. Although he couldn't quite understand why, the King offered them a chance to return to their city, rebuild the temple (do you remember the temple Solomon built?) and take as much gold as they needed.

The people were very happy to see good old Jerusalem again, and they soon set to work on the temple which the Babylonians had knocked down.

It took six years to complete it, and when it was finished it was just as good as ever. God looked down at the temple and gave a little smile. 'My house,' He thought.

Years later, a Jew named Nehemiah happened to ask a friend of his how things were in Jerusalem. The friend told sadly of the broken remains of the city. 'The temple is rebuilt, but you should see the walls, the burnt gates – terrible state.'

Nehemiah had a long think about this, and the more he thought, the more sad he became. 'What can I do?' he wondered.

Then he had an idea. He was friendly with the King, so he went to him and asked him a favour.

'I could rebuild the walls of Jerusalem with your help, and the help of God,' he said.

The King agreed, and supplied Nehemiah with money, lots of men, and the names of brick and wood sellers he could use.

When Nehemiah got to the remains of Jerusalem it made him very sad. The once beautiful city was all in pieces.

But soon every man around was helping with the rebuilding, and even the ladies did their bit – bringing sandwiches and drinks for the workers. They all worked so hard that they almost forgot about going to sleep. They worked and worked until the job was completed, and Jerusalem looked beautiful again.

It was almost as if Nehemiah and his men knew that God had planned a great happening for the city. A little boy was going to be born near there soon . . . but you'll hear about that later.

JONAH AND THE WHALE

This is one of the last, and most exciting stories in the Old Testament. It all goes to prove once again that God always wanted to look after his people; not only the special ones like Moses and David, but everyone.

Jonah was a good man. God watched him from behind a big cloud, and decided that he was the man to go and sort out the people of Nineveh. (They were very wicked and had offended God.)

But surprisingly when God had a word with Jonah, the poor old man was so scared that he packed his bags, paid the rent, and scuttled down to the harbour as fast as he could. There he found a ship to take him away. (Fancy running away from God – that's silly isn't it?)

As the ship left the harbour, Jonah went downstairs, thinking all the time that he just wasn't strong or good enough to do God's work at Nineveh.

He sat huddled among the crates of grain and barrels of oil, wondering if God would know where he was.

Of course God knew. He sent a mighty wind across the sea, and the ship started bobbing about like a sponge in a bath. All the men were scared, 'What are we going to do?' they cried. 'What is to become of us?'

In those early days they had some funny ideas. They immediately thought that someone on the ship was unlucky. After questioning everyone, they decided that Jonah was definitely the man who had caused all the trouble, so as the ship dipped and tumbled in the furious sea, old Jonah was thrown overboard.

Immediately the sea became completely calm. The sun came out and the black clouds and wild white topped waves disappeared completely.

Jonah's troubles certainly weren't over. He had only been floating a few seconds when an enormous whale came along,

6

opened its great mouth, and swallowed the helpless Jonah.

The old man really couldn't understand what was happening. It didn't seem so long ago that he was sitting at home, and now here he was inside a whale.

It was terribly cold, and very, very dark. He looked up and all he could see was the pinky inside of the great whale, and occasionally a little light from the huge tooth-covered mouth.

Jonah sat on the bottom of the whale's stomach wondering what to do.

As you have probably guessed, all these goings on were done by God. He really wanted Jonah to have a word with the people of Nineveh, and when the old man had run away, God thought this was the best way to bring him back.

The whale answered Jonah's call for some way of escape. The great creature opened its mouth, and out popped Jonah, right on to a sandy beach.

He rubbed the water from his eyes, and was just in time to see the big old whale disappearing out to sea.

Jonah was wide eyed with amazement as he muttered, 'Thanks for the lift.'

He turned round to see where he was, and to his surprise saw the city of Nineveh right in front of him. 'The Lord has delivered me to Nineveh,' he thought. 'I will obey him in future, it's much less trouble.'

The old man clambered to his feet, and walked towards the city he was going to sort out.

As the Old Testament comes to an end, you can understand more and more how God wanted his people to be. He didn't want them to give him presents, he didn't want them to stop eating to show their love, all he wanted was to teach them to care for each other. He wanted his world to live in peace, follow his commandments, and have faith. Remember that.

THE NEW TESTAMENT

MARY HAS A BABY

Mary was sitting in the sun outside her house. It was a normal day, a bit of cooking, a bit of helping round the house. She was having a few minutes rest when suddenly an angel appeared. 'Are you Mary?' he asked. 'Yes, who are you?' the startled girl replied. 'I am an angel from God, and I have a surprise for you – you're going to have a baby.' Mary raised her hand to her mouth. 'It would be a surprise, I'm not even married.'

The angel knew that Mary was going to marry Joseph. He explained the details. 'Your child will be the son of God, he will be loved throughout the world for thousands of years.' Mary thought she was dreaming. 'It is hard to understand,' she said hesitantly, 'what shall I call the baby?'

'His name is Jesus,' the angel answered. 'Now I must fly.' And he was gone.

Mary sat for a very long time without saying anything. She thought about all the angel had said, and she prayed a nice thank you to God.

'Jesus,' she thought. 'That's a nice name.'

Mary married Joseph, and they both left for Bethlehem, where they were going to live.

They had to travel a long way, so Mary rode on a donkey while Joseph walked beside her.

They arrived in the town at nightfall, and Joseph asked if there was somewhere to stay, because his wife was going to have a baby. Someone said, 'Try the inn, they rent out rooms.'

They walked down the quiet streets, Joseph worrying about his wife, and Mary feeling more and more tired.

'Here we are,' said Joseph. He told Mary to wait outside while he went in to arrange things.

A few minutes later, a miserable Joseph came out. 'There's no room at the inn.'

The couple sadly left the town, and found a cattle shed to sleep in.

During the night Mary had her baby, and said to Joseph, 'He shall be named Jesus,' Joseph nodded. 'Lovely,' he said.

Not so far away, there were shepherds looking after their sheep. The angel suddenly appeared, and the shepherds looked surprised. The angel said, 'Don't worry. I've come to tell you some happy news. The Son of God has been born in Bethlehem tonight, go and see him.'

To the amazement of the shepherds, the sky was filled with angels singing. 'Glory to God, and peace to all men.'

'Come on lads,' said one of the shepherds, 'Let's go and have a look.'

They found Mary, Joseph and little Jesus just as the angel had said, and while the sheep and cows looked on, the men all prayed to God. The baby lay asleep in a manger, with lots of warm clothes to cover him.

In those days there was a King called Herod. He got to hear of Jesus and was worried about it. 'King of the Jews, eh?' (For that is what Jesus was called) 'I'll give him "King of the Jews." Not if I've got anything to do with it.'

He heard that three wise men were going to visit Jesus. They had seen a very bright star in the night sky, and were going to follow it. They knew that it was shining right over the manger.

'Go and find where he is,' Herod said to the wise men. 'I want to worship him.' As the three men left, Herod chuckled to himself. 'Worship him!' he laughed. 'Get rid of him, more like. King of the Jews indeed. I'm King of the Jews.'

He looked out of the window and shouted to the three wise men, 'Hurry back, I can't wait to worship Jesus.'

What a nasty man.

The three wise men travelled at night, following the bright star. Finally they arrived, and gave the baby Jesus lots of presents. There was gold, and frankincense and myrrh to make him smell nice.

The men worshipped Jesus, and thanked God for sending him to the world.

They were just going to go back home when God said,

'Don't tell Herod where Jesus is. He wants to hurt him, not worship him.'

'Right,' said the three wise men. 'We'll go back a different way.'

And they did, so Herod never found out where Jesus was.

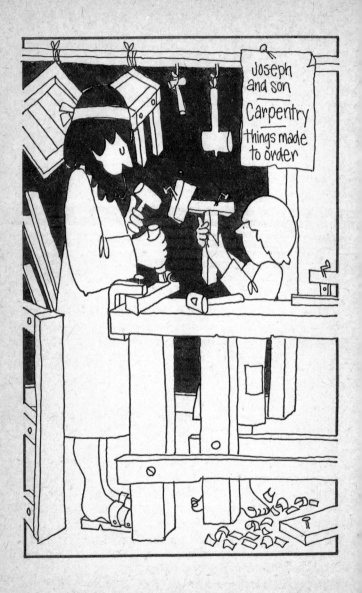

Joseph
and son
—
Carpentry
—
things made
to order

JESUS GROWS UP

Herod was obviously still very interested in finding Jesus, to make sure he was never crowned King of the Jews.

God was watching very carefully, and one night when Joseph was asleep, he heard God tell him to leave Israel and go to Egypt, because Jesus would be safe there.

Early the next morning, before the sun had come over the trees, Joseph and his family did exactly as God suggested.

They lived in Egypt for a while, until naughty King Herod died, and then they returned to live in Nazareth. There, in the warm sun, the young Jesus helped his father in his carpentry business. He learnt how to make tables and window frames, and Joseph taught him the best way to saw wood, hammer in nails, and drill holes.

When Jesus was twelve, Mary and Joseph took him to a big festival in Jerusalem. All the people who lived in Nazareth went to it, so when they started home the boy's parents thought he must be at the front of all the people with some friends.

It took Mary and Joseph a long time to realise that Jesus had stayed behind in Jerusalem.

They were terribly worried as they returned to look for him, but finally they found where he was. Do you know where? He was in the temple, which is a bit like a church, with all the teachers and vicars of the town.

He was talking about all sorts of things, and they were all listening intently. He spoke about God, and all the wonderful things of nature, and the more he talked, the more they listened. The teachers were amazed – here was a boy of twelve talking with as much knowledge as they had.

When Mary and Joseph arrived they said what any Mummy and Daddy would say. 'Why do you behave like this, you should have known we'd worry about you.'

Jesus, who was always a good and obedient boy, said, 'Why

did you look for me? You know I have to do my Father's business.'

His parents didn't know quite what he meant, but they thought it must have something to do with God. They said goodbye to the wise men of the temple, and started home to Nazareth.

As Jesus grew up he became more clever, until everyone wanted to hear him and find out what he thought about things.

Jesus gave the people hope for the future, and although all this happened nearly two thousand years ago, people still find hope and happiness from the stories of Jesus.

Read on — you'll find out why.

THE DEVIL TRIES TO TURN
JESUS AGAINST GOD

When Jesus had grown up he decided it was time to prove to God that he was a good son, good enough to be the person who told everyone about Heaven.

One day he walked into the wilderness, determined to stay there for forty days and forty nights without eating.

Needless to say, after a while Jesus got very hungry. He thought of bread and butter, and fish, and all the things he really liked. 'But I'm not going to eat,' he thought to himself. 'I shall not eat until I get out of the wilderness.'

Now in the stories so far there have been some very bad people, just think of Joseph's brothers, and Herod. But there was never anyone so bad, nasty and utterly horrid as the devil, and this was the time he decided to make an entrance.

Jesus was sitting on a rock looking into the sky, when the devil flew up and perched just next to him.

'Hello,' he said. Jesus was surprised (who wouldn't be?). The devil continued, 'If you are the real son of God, turn these stones into bread, and eat it.'

Although Jesus was hungry, he said, 'Go away, you horrible thing. I don't live on bread, I live on the words of God.'

The devil was tempting Jesus. In other words, he was trying to persuade him to do bad things in front of God. The devil hoped that God would be angry with Jesus, and lose interest in him.

It didn't work for the devil the first time he tried, so he had another go. He lifted Jesus right into the air, and balanced him on the very top point of the temple in the town nearby.

'Now, Jesus. If you're the Son of God, leap off; your friendly angels are bound to catch you before you hit the ground.' The devil roared with laughter. 'Go on, bet you can't.'

Jesus got angry. 'Now listen here, you,' he shouted. 'You should never tempt God.'

The devil became depressed. 'Nothing seems to be work-

ing,' he thought. 'He won't be tempted to do anything wrong,
I'm fed up.' And he was.

After a while the devil returned to Jesus, who by that time
was back in the wilderness again, and said, 'Follow me.'

The wicked devil took Jesus to a very high mountain, and
waved his hand majestically at all the lakes, forests and towns
in the sunny landscape.

'All this!' he cried. 'All this will be yours, if you just do one
little thing.'

Jesus asked what it was.

'Fall down and worship me,' said the devil, pointing a
horny finger at himself.

'You?' exclaimed Jesus. 'Never! Get away from me. People
should worship God, and no one else. Go away.'

The devil shrugged his shoulders, snarled a couple of times,
and crept away. The temptation hadn't worked.

We're all tempted with nice things, and it takes a strong person
to say no; but if you do what you know to be right, it's always
better in the end.

WATER? NO, IT'S WINE!

When Jesus really started teaching people about God and
Heaven, he chose some men to travel with him. They were
called the disciples. You probably won't remember all their
names, but here are some of them – Simon, and Andrew his
brother, and James and John, who were also brothers. As they
all journeyed together, Jesus did lots of wonderful things
called miracles – things that no one else could ever do. We
know how he did them, don't we? God helped him.

Jesus and the disciples had been invited to a wedding in Cana
of Galilee.

Everybody was having a great time, eating and drinking
and dancing about. Suddenly someone said, 'There's no more
wine.'

Everyone stopped dancing and groaned. Mary, the mother of Jesus was there, and she turned to her son and said, 'Can't you do something?' Jesus thought for a moment. 'Bring those waterpots over here,' he said, 'make sure they're nice and full.'

The servants did just as he said, they filled up the pots with water, and stood them in front of Jesus.

'Now,' said Jesus. 'Take a cup of the water, and let the master taste it.'

The man took a sip. 'It's wine!' he cried. 'It's lovely wine! It's much nicer than the wine we had at the beginning of the wedding!'

The disciples turned to Jesus and smiled. 'Changing water into wine – that's a real miracle,' they said.

Jesus looked at them, and gave a little smile up to the sky.

JESUS HEALS SICK PEOPLE

To show everyone just how wonderful God was, Jesus spent a lot of his time in different towns healing people.

There was a man who had an evil spirit. He couldn't help it, he was just like that. One day when Jesus was in the church, this man said, 'Why don't you go away, Jesus, and leave us alone.'

Jesus just looked at him and said, 'The devil is in you.' Then he spoke to the devil. 'Leave this man immediately.'

After that the man was well again, and everyone started talking about Jesus.

In this way he cured many people. People with bad hands, people with diseases. They were all well after Jesus had finished.

As you can imagine, hundreds of people wanted to see Jesus, just so they could touch him. There was one man who was far too ill to walk, let alone push through the crowds to see him. The man's friends got some rope, and lowered him in his bed through a hole in the roof. He landed next to Jesus, who said, 'You are healed. Pick up your bed, and walk.' And he did.

The law men of the towns were getting tired of Jesus. Up to that time people used to think they were the greatest, now they thought Jesus was. The bad black-robed men put their heads together to try and find a way to get rid of him.

JESUS TALKS TO THE PEOPLE ON THE MOUNTAIN

As Jesus continued his work, he collected a lot more disciples. Out of these followers he chose twelve to be his very special people. He called them the apostles. There was Peter, Andrew, James and John, Phillip, Bartholomew, Thomas, Matthew, another James, Lebbeus, Simon and Judas. (Remember that name – you'll see why later.)

Jesus and his apostles climbed high on to a mountain one day, and all the people followed them. Jesus sat down on a big rock, crossed his legs, and began to talk to them.

It was a very long talk, and he said lots of things worth remembering.

He said that almost everyone was blessed by God – sad people who need comforting, timid people, and anyone who wants to be good.

Kind and pure people would have a chance to see God, and peace makers would be called the children of God. Those who were punished by unbelieving men for saying they loved God would be all right in the end, because they would go to Heaven.

Jesus said, 'Even if you don't like someone very much, you should still be nice to them, and help them. You mustn't steal and you mustn't be jealous.' After that Jesus taught everybody the Lord's prayer, which you probably know, and he suggested that the people should say it to themselves when they had a quiet moment in the day.

When Jesus had finished speaking, all the people turned to each other and started saying things like, 'He's much more

clever than the law men and priests,' and, 'I could listen to him for hours.'

As the sun set, hundreds of people climbed down the mountain and returned happily to their homes.

Jesus felt pretty happy, too.

JESUS TELLS THE STORM
TO CALM DOWN

Jesus went back to his home town to see how things were going. On Sunday he went to church and read to the town people.

They all agreed he was trying to be a bit too clever, and they got very angry. 'What's this young carpenter doing, telling us all his smart ideas?' They cried, and they grabbed him and started to march him out of town.

Jesus said, 'What are you doing? Why is it that everyone thinks I'm sensible apart from you lot? Let me go.'

There were so many people in the end Jesus just walked through them, for half of them didn't know what they were meant to be doing, and he left town.

Jesus and his followers decided to go sailing. The idea was to visit a man who was ill on the other side of the lake.

They all climbed into the boat and set off. Well, it was a hot day, and Jesus hadn't gone to bed very early the night before, so he fell asleep.

As he slept the water started to get rough. The men looked at each other glumly. 'Oh dear,' said one, 'there's going to be a storm, look at those clouds.'

He was right. The sky got blacker, and the wind got stronger, and the boat seemed to be bobbing up and down so much that it sometimes went under the waves.

'Help!' they cried, 'we're going to be drowned! We're lost!' The men moaned and groaned so loudly that they woke Jesus. He sat up straight, looked round, and jumped to the front of the boat. 'Stop it,' he shouted at the sea and the sky, 'what do you think you're doing? How dare you?'

The sea flattened so quickly that all the men in the boat fell over. The sun came out, and all the clouds blew away.

The wide eyed men sat up and looked at Jesus. Jesus looked

back. 'Haven't you any faith?' he said. 'Have faith, and you don't have to worry about that sort of thing. Remember that.'

And it goes without saying that they did.

JESUS FEEDS 5,000 PEOPLE AND WALKS ON WATER

One day Jesus was feeling a bit sad, so he walked to a quiet place with the apostles.

By this time Jesus was getting well known, so thousands of people followed him to the quiet place.

Soon it wasn't very quiet any more. Everyone was talking, and getting excited, and asking questions. The people were like sheep, making a fuss of their shepherd.

When Jesus had finished talking it was getting late. One of the apostles said, 'I'm starving, and so is everyone else. Shall we go into town for something to eat?'

Jesus thought for a moment. 'No, we'll eat here. How much food has everyone got?'

The apostles asked all the people what they had. No one had anything, except one small boy who had five loaves of bread and two small fishes.

'That won't go very far,' one of the apostles said. 'That will only feed two of us.' Jesus looked up 'We'll feed everyone here, all five thousand of them.'

The apostles looked amazed. 'You must be joking,' they said. 'They'll only get half a mouthful each.'

'Wait and see,' said Jesus, knowing that God would help out.

None of the apostles quite knew what happened next. Suddenly there was enough bread and fish for everyone. In fact, there was so much that they collected twelve baskets of left overs.

When everyone realised what had happened, they prayed with Jesus, thanking God for their lovely meal.

After all the people had gone home, Jesus sent the apostles ahead of him to the boat they kept at the lake. He sat by himself and did some thinking. When it was just beginning to get dark, he strolled down to the shore and, seeing his apostles in their boat, decided to walk out to them. Now anyone else who tries to walk on water soon sinks, but Jesus was different. He actually walked on top of the water, all the way to the boat.

Well, as you have probably guessed, the apostles were rather shocked to see a lone figure approaching out of the mist towards them.

They didn't realise it was Jesus at first, and they all cried, 'It's a nasty spirit, we'll be drowned!' But Jesus, who was still completely dry, said, 'It's only me, lads. Don't worry.'

The apostles calmed down. 'Jesus, you did give us a shock – how did you do that?'

Jesus smiled his God's-helping-me smile, and said, 'It's simple, all you need is a bit of faith. Peter, walk over to me.'

Peter looked a little apprehensive, but since Jesus said it, he thought he would be all right. He stepped out of the boat, and found he could actually walk on the water!

He grinned a rather watery grin at Jesus, and walked a few steps further. Just at that moment, Peter thought, 'This is ridiculous, how can I be walking on water? It's impossible.'

Well, that thought was the same as losing faith, so you know what happened? Peter started sinking. He was just about up to his knees when Jesus held out his hand and gently lifted him up again.

'You must have faith, Peter,' he said. 'Everyone sinks without faith.'

The apostles knew what Jesus meant by that. Have faith and you'll be all right. Simple, isn't it?

JESUS TELLS THE STORY OF THE GOOD SAMARITAN

A lawman was sitting, cross legged, listening to Jesus talking about God and Heaven, and how kind people should be.

He suddenly stood up, and said, 'Jesus, who is my neighbour?' He didn't mean who was the person who lived next door, Jesus probably wouldn't have known that. What he did mean was, 'who can I trust as a friend?'

Jesus smiled. 'A lot of people ask me that, I'll tell you a little story, and at the end of it I will ask you who the man's neighbour was.' (You try and guess too.)

The people gathered round to hear. They loved the stories that Jesus told. He began, 'A man left Jerusalem one day to start on a long journey. He had lots of food, money and nice clothes with him. He was walking along, whistling to himself in the sunshine when suddenly a band of naughty robbers leapt out from behind some bushes, and banged this poor man on the head. He fell over, and the robbers stole his money, and all his clothes. They ran away laughing, leaving the man flat out on the roadside. He really felt very ill, and he just couldn't move.

'Later, a priest came down the road and, seeing the man lying there, do you know what he did?'

The crowd all looked at each other. 'Did he pick him up and give him a drink?' asked one. 'Did he call for help?' asked another.

'No,' said Jesus. 'He just passed by on the other side of the road. He thought the robbers might bang him on the head too, so he hurried away. The same thing happened when another man came along. He too passed by on the other side of the road.

'Luckily for the wounded man, a Samaritan (he's from Samaria) came past. He saw the poor fellow lying there, and felt very sorry for him. He jumped off his donkey and gave the man a drink, bandaged up his head, and gave him a lift

into town. The Samaritan stopped at the inn, and got the best room for the man to stay in.

'He told the innkeeper to give the wounded man everything he wanted, and gave him some money for his trouble.

'Now, which of the three men on that road was a good neighbour?'

Well, of course, everybody knew the answer – it was the Samaritan. He made quite sure that the man, whom he had never met before, was safe and comfortable. And as Jesus said, 'If everybody did that, this world would be a much better place to live in.'

He was right, wasn't he?

THE SON WHO WASTED HIS MONEY

Jesus talked a lot about forgiving, and forgetting if people have hurt you. He told a very good story about the son of a rich man.

The boy was helping with the sheep, and doing lots of jobs round the house that he didn't enjoy very much. One day he got so bored that he asked his father, 'If anything happens to you, I get a lot of your money, don't I?' The father said, 'Of course you do, Why?' The boy said that if it was all the same to the old man, he would like his money right away. The father was a bit sad to think his son was going to leave home, but he said, 'Very well. If that's what you want, here you are.' And he gave the boy a big bag of money.

The naughty son packed his bags and left for another country. There he had a whale of a time. He ate at all the smart restaurants, went out with girls, and bought all sorts of lovely things. He had such a wonderful time wasting all his money that very soon he had none left.

He had to sell his chariot so he could pay for food, and all the girls he knew didn't talk to him any more because now he hadn't any money.

He had been very silly.

The boy finally had to get a job feeding pigs, and he was so hungry he felt like eating the pig food. But he didn't. Instead he said to himself, 'My dad's servants get enough to eat. I think I'll go home and say – I'm sorry, and I'm no longer good enough to be called your son, but can I work with your servants?'

So he did. As he walked towards the house, his father saw him coming and ran to meet him. 'Hi! How are you?' he shouted. 'Nice to see you!'

The wasteful son looked sad. 'I'm sorry,' he said, 'I'm no longer good enough to be called your son, but can I work with your servants . . . please?'

'Nonsense!' cried the old man, 'Wouldn't hear of it!' And he scuttled into the house to find some nice clothes for his son.

While he was there, he told cook to make the best meal she could, because there was going to be a party.

Meanwhile, another son of the old man was looking after the sheep. He heard all the music, and as he looked down at the house, he saw lights flickering and people dancing.

When he got home and heard what had happened he was furious. 'I stay here doing all the work,' he shouted, 'and my silly money-wasting brother comes back and gets all the treatment. It's not fair.' He stamped his foot and walked away.

His old father ran after him and said, 'Son, everything I've got is yours now, because your brother has had his share. So be kind, I thought he was dead and he's alive. I thought we'd lost him and now we've found him. Come on, come and join in the fun.'

So he did, and the party went on so long that it was nearly morning before they all got to bed.

Jesus told his friends that this story showed how to forgive. The old father could quite easily have told his naughty son to go away, but he didn't. He was kind and forgiving – and Jesus liked that in a person.

JESUS IN TROUBLE

Jesus carried on his good work. He helped and cured people, and was nice to unpopular men. One of these men was Zaccheus. Although the people of Jericho didn't like him, he was still one of the followers of Jesus. Zaccheus was very small, so when Jesus was there he couldn't see through the crowds to find out what he was saying. As he tried to peep through, the people said, 'Go away Zaccheus,' and 'why don't you go home?'

Finally the poor little fellow climbed a tree to see better.

'What are you doing up there?' Jesus asked.

'I wanted to see you,' was the reply.

Much to the surprise of the crowd, Jesus not only talked to Zaccheus, but actually asked himself to lunch with the man.

Zaccheus jumped out of the tree and said, 'Marvellous! You're very welcome!'

Jesus heard all the people saying, 'He's going to lunch with a sinner!' and 'What's he doing going round with baddies?'

But Jesus didn't mind. He knew that Zaccheus was good really, and he was nice to people. Jesus said, 'You're all right Zaccheus, besides we're all sons of Abraham, aren't we?'

He patted the little man on the back, and they walked away to have a lovely lunch together.

All the things that Jesus had been up to were really annoying those priests you heard about in an earlier story. They had meetings in secret, and finally decided that Jesus had to go.

'Shall we put him in prison?' said one. 'Shall we stop him speaking in public?' asked another.

'No,' said Caiaphas, who was the head priest. 'He is too dangerous. The people like him more than they like us. He must die.'

So it was decided. The Son of God, who was only interested in being kind and helping people was to die. Jesus was to be blamed for something, arrested, and stopped from talking about God forever.

The cruel men began to work out their evil plan.

Jesus realised that he was in trouble. He kept away from the priests, because he knew they would catch him if they had half a chance. Because of this, he didn't go to a special feast in Jerusalem, which annoyed the priests, because they wanted to catch him there.

Instead he stayed with his friends, where he was safe, and they looked after him.

One night at supper, a girl called Mary produced a pot of ointment. It was really expensive and had a lovely smell. She poured it over the feet of Jesus, and smoothed it in gently with her hair.

One of the disciples, Judas, said, 'What on earth are you doing? We could have got lots of money for that ointment. We could have bought things for the poor people.' He looked very angry, but Jesus didn't agree with him. 'There will always be poor people needing help,' he said, 'but I won't be with you for ever. In fact, I won't be with you much longer.'

Mary had only done this because she loved Jesus, and wanted to show him she cared.

Jesus appreciated that.

JESUS ARRIVES AT JERUSALEM

A little while later, Jesus rode into Jerusalem on a donkey. When he was approaching the city, all his followers came running to meet him. There were hundreds of them, all waving palm leaves and laughing and laying down their coats for him to ride over.

It was a very happy occasion. Jesus was delighted to see that the people still loved him, and the people were pleased to see Jesus again.

Some of the bad men said, 'Why don't you stop them getting so excited, Jesus?' He replied, 'No! It's such a wonderful day that if no one was here, all the stones in the street would cheer and praise God!'

Everybody thought he was wonderful. They shouted, 'Jesus! He's the greatest!'

Later on that day he walked down to the temple to pray. When he arrived he found that all the shopkeepers and money lenders had set up a sort of market place, and the people of the city were buying things, arguing and bargaining with each other.

Jesus was furious. 'This is a house of prayer,' he shouted, 'and you have turned it into a meeting place for robbers!'

He kicked over the stalls, stamped on all the clothes they were selling, and released all the animals. He grabbed the traders by the collars and marched them into the street.

After that Jesus walked back to the temple, 'Now, where were we?'

He began healing people, and helping anyone who was unhappy. This, of course, was too much for the bad priests who wanted to kill Jesus. 'Let's grab him now,' they whispered, 'let's get him.'

But all bullies are very scared really, and these men were no exception. They decided it was better not to try and catch

116

Jesus at that time, because all his followers might throw them out of town. They sneaked away, and vowed to get him at the very next opportunity.

JUDAS TELLS THE BAD MEN ABOUT JESUS

One of the disciples, Judas, was standing in the temple doing nothing in particular, when he heard someone mention Jesus.

He crept a little closer to hear what they were saying. It was the bad priests, they were trying to decide how they could catch Jesus, and get rid of him. Judas walked up to them and said a very surprising thing. He said, 'How much will you give me if I tell you where Jesus is?' Very surprising, because Judas was meant to be one of the friends of Jesus, and he was actually trying to make money from giving away a friend. Of course the baddies were delighted. They smiled and nudged each other and said, 'Judas, we will give you a lot of money if you let us know where to find Jesus, but it must be a very quiet place because we're scared of crowds.'

It was all arranged – naughty Judas would let the priests know in good time, so they could capture Jesus and take him away.

THE LAST SUPPER TOGETHER

Jesus had arranged a very special supper for his disciples. He invited everyone, including Peter and that no-good Judas.

It wasn't a very happy occasion, Jesus was saying that it was the very last supper they would have together, and Judas was feeling so guilty that he couldn't eat.

Jesus picked up the bread and said, 'Eat this, it is my body,' and then he got some wine and said, 'drink this, it's my blood.'

By the time Jesus had said that it was the last meal he would have before he went to Heaven, everyone was so sad that they couldn't eat any more.

Jesus stood up and announced that he was going to wash everyone's feet. Peter didn't think it was right for him to do this, because it was the job of a servant. Jesus insisted. He said, 'I want to serve people, and so should you.'

What Jesus was doing was making his men clean in the eyes of God.

'You are all clean now,' he said after a while, 'except one.' He glanced at Judas, who thought. 'He knows I'm going to betray him. How can he know?'

Jesus did know about Judas, because he knew everything about his future, including his death at the hands of the bad men.

He turned to his disciples. 'One of you,' he said, 'is going to betray me, going to tell my killers where I am.'

The disciples all cried, 'We wouldn't do that, Jesus. We wouldn't let you down.'

And Judas said, 'No, not your old pals.'

Jesus picked up a piece of bread from the table. He held it up. 'I am going to dip this bread in a bowl, and whoever I give it to, is the man who is going to betray me.'

The disciples looked sad as Jesus handed the bread to Judas.

'Go and do what you have to do,' said Jesus.

Judas jumped up, crying, and ran out of the house.

Jesus sat down and looked round at his dearest friends.

'I will be leaving you soon,' he said, 'and where I am going you will come eventually.

'Before I go, I will leave you with another commandment – love one another. Friends are the greatest thing God has ever given you, so treat them well, and love them truly.

'Don't worry about anything, because God is there to look after you. Remember that.'

As he got up, Peter said, 'Jesus, I will love you always.'

Jesus said, 'Are you sure? Before tomorrow morning you will say that you never knew me, and you will say it three times.'

'I won't!' cried Peter.

'Wait and see,' said Jesus.

IN THE GARDEN OF GETHSEMANE

After supper Jesus and his disciples walked to a quiet place they knew. It was the garden of Gethsemane.

It was very dark, and Jesus said to his friends, 'Wait with me. I want to say a prayer to God.'

The disciples sat down as Jesus knelt to speak to God. He knew that it was nearly time to be captured, and he asked his father in Heaven for extra strength to stand it. He knew that, at that very moment, Judas was hurrying to the garden with the bad priests and some soldiers.

When Jesus had finished praying, he returned to his men, but they were all asleep.

He woke them, saying, 'My time has come, please wait with me.'

There was a sound of running feet. Judas and the soldiers burst through the bushes waving swords. 'Which one is Jesus?' shouted the commander. Judas ran to Jesus and kissed him, to show which man it was.

'Judas,' said Jesus, 'you have betrayed me with a kiss.'

The disciples began to draw their swords, but Jesus told them not to – he would go quietly.

The Son of God was lead away at the hands of soldiers, who didn't really know what they were doing.

Just before morning, Peter was wandering through the streets. A man walked up to him and said, 'Aren't you one of the friends of Jesus?'

'No,' said Peter, afraid that he would be arrested too.

It was a cold night, so he walked over to some men who were making a fire.

'Good evening,' they said. 'Evening,' replied Peter, absent-mindedly. A woman was staring at him. 'Aren't you one of the Jesus lot?'

Peter looked nervous, 'Course not, never met him in my life.'

Another man walked up to Peter. 'You're a friend of that Jesus aren't you?' he said.

'No, no, no. I'm not!' shouted Peter.

At that moment it was morning, and the cock in a nearby farm crowed loudly.

'I've done what Jesus said I would do,' thought Peter, 'I've said I didn't know him . . . three times.'

When he realised what he had done, he wept bitterly for his friend.

PILATE AND THE TRIAL

The next morning the captive Jesus was brought before Pilate, the Roman Governor.

By this time the priests had turned the people against Jesus. They were shouting, 'Kill him! Put him on a cross! Crucify him!'

Pilate looked at Jesus, 'Are you the King of the Jews?'

'That's what everybody says,' answered Jesus. 'But I come from somewhere else.'

Pilate looked over the balcony of his house at all the people. 'This man has done nothing,' he shouted. 'How can he be crucified?'

The crowds shouted louder and louder. The bad priests who had started all the trouble smiled at each other. Their plan had worked.

'Right!' declared Pilate. 'Have it your own way. Kill him, but I wash my hands of it!'

He took a bowl of water and dipped his hands into it, showing that the matter was no longer anything to do with him.

The soldiers grabbed Jesus and beat him. They made a crown out of some thorny twigs and stuck it on his head. All the people shouted, 'Hooray for the King of the Jews!' They were being really nasty.

A great wooden cross was put on the back of Jesus, and the sad figure walked through the streets, burdened by the heavy cross. The crowd laughed and shouted. They had quite forgotten how they once loved Jesus, and how he helped so many people.

The blood-stained figure climbed to the top of a hill, and there they nailed him to the cross.

As the Son of God began to die, the crowd looked on . . .

JESUS DIES ON THE CROSS

On the hillside there were three crosses. Jesus was in the middle, with a robber on either side.

As they were dying, the robbers asked Jesus, 'If you are the Son of God, why can't you free us all?'

Jesus looked up to Heaven. 'Dear God,' he said, 'why have you forgotten me?'

Jesus couldn't understand why he should end this way, after devoting his life to the love of God, and helping his fellow men.

'Forgive them all,' he sighed, 'they don't really know what they are doing.'

As his strength began to leave him, the sky grew darker and darker. In the orangy twilight he became thirsty, so a kind soldier filled a sponge with vinegar and held it to his mouth.

His few remaining friends sat at the base of his cross, looking up at their beloved companion, and remembering how he had helped the people who now turned against him.

As Jesus got weaker, there was a grumbling sound from the ground. The sky became completely black, and cracks formed in the hillside and through the city. The people looked at each other, 'This is a signal from God, this man is the Son of God.' They were fearful because of what they had done.

Thunder rolled, lightning flashed and the very earth seemed to break in two.

'God!' shouted Jesus, 'My spirit is in your hands!'

The heavens opened, and torrential rain fell on the place where the Son of God was dying. Jesus moved on the cross, shut his eyes and murmured, 'It is finished . . .'

JESUS RETURNS TO HIS DISCIPLES

The body of Jesus was put in a cave in the hillside, with a big stone to cover it. Soldiers were sent to guard the cave in case anyone tried to get in.

Three days after the crucifixion, Mary went to the cave. As she stood there, the angel of God appeared and opened the entrance.

Jesus had gone.

'Don't be afraid,' said the angel, 'he has risen to Heaven.'

For the next forty days, before he finally returned to Heaven, Jesus appeared to his disciples many times. They couldn't believe it was him at first, but after he had shown them the scars on his hands and feet, they knew their master had returned to them.

He told them the meaning of the bible stories, and filled them with the glorious works of God. He prepared his friends for spreading his words to the world. They talked of the miracles, and the healing, and the stories Jesus had told in his lifetime.

They talked of teaching goodness to everyone. To their friends, to their enemies, and every man in the world. Not only in those days of the distant past, but today, when people need the goodness of God just as much.

The friends sat together, as they had so many times before, and talked of the three things that were most important to Jesus, and to you. The three things that he left us in those early days of our world – love, peace, and of course . . . faith.